ORACLES OF WISDOM

a mini book for a mega life!

GBEMINIYI EBODA

ORACLES OF WISDOM

A Mini Book For A Mega Life!

Oracles of Wisdom by Gbeminiyi Eboda

First printed in 2004

Second Print 2009

Third print 2015

Requests for permission should be made in writing to

Move Your World Int'l

email: info@moveurworld.com

phone: +234 (0)809 827 5777

Design: GreenKnight Solutions.

www.moveyourworld.com

CONTENT

INTRODUCTION

You are an addition to this generation,
a plus factor to our world.
Our world will be incomplete in the
absence of your contributions.
Therefore, your existence deserves to
be maximized.
Welcome to your season of
unlimited exploits!

DISCOVERY AND UNIQUENESS

It takes living with authenticity to become an authority and your authenticity lies in your originality.

Except they give a distinction in the sounds, how shall it be known what is piped or harped?
1Cor 14:7

Failure is supposed to be a teacher, not a killer, a trial of your faith, not its burial.

For a just man falleth seven times, and riseth up again; but the wicked shall fall into mischief.
Prov 24:16

Power is the ability to walk away from what you desire to protect what you have discovered.

But Daniel purposed in his heart that he would not defile himself with the portion of the king's meat, nor with the wine which he drank: therefore he requested of the prince of the eunuchs that he might not defile himself.
Dan 1:8

So many people live on borrowed identities and bury their own, whatever you borrow, you must return. If the whole world were to be like someone, the world would be boring. There is celebration in uniqueness. Be yourself!

Let every man abide in the same calling wherein he was called.
1Cor 7:20

Entry into the world is the genesis of existence; discovery of the purpose of existence, is the genesis of life.

Then said I, Lo, I come (in the volume of the book it is written of me,) to do thy will, O God.
Heb 10:7

Life's value does not lie in how much of it has been lived, but in how much of it has been filled.

I have fought the good fight of faith, I have FINISHED my course, I have kept the faith.
2Tim 4:7

What you behold continually is what you will become eventually.

But we all ,with open face beholding as in a glass the glory of the Lord, are changed into the same image from glory to glory. Even as the spirit of the Lord.
2Cor 3:18

Until you dare to be different, you cannot make a difference.

Except they give a distinction in the sounds, how shall it be known what is piped or harped.
1Cor 14:7

Know yourself, be yourself and be the best, God will do the rest.

Let every man, wherein he is called therein abide with God.
1Cor 7:24

MATURITY AND PROGRESS

Pride sees what has been done, Love sees what can be done.

...but this one thing I do, forgetting those things which are behind and reaching forth unto those things which are before.
Phil 3:13

We must never mistake progress for arrival. The best is yet to come, keep on keeping on.

Arise ye, depart, for this is not your rest.
Micah 2:10

If Jesus is the captain of your life, you will definitely arrive at the shore of fulfillment.

Being confident of this very thing, that he which hath begun a good work in you will perform it until the day of Jesus Christ.
Phil 1:6

Nobody goes forward looking backward and nobody goes backward looking forward.

...but this one thing I do, forgetting those things which are behind and reaching forth unto those things which are before.
Phil 3:13

The Evidence of life is growth, the proof of life is progress, where progress is absent, life is in doubt.

...and Jesus increased in wisdom and stature, and in favour with God and man.
Luke 2:52

There is a difference between boldness and pride, and there is a difference between meekness and timidity.

Blessed are the meek; for they shall inherit the earth .
Matt 5:5

Never try to own what
will make you owe,
Indebtedness is a curse!

Owe no man anything.
Romans 13:8

FAMILY LIFE AND MARRIAGE

It is good for a woman to have a pretty face, but it is far better for her to have a prettier faith.

Whose adorning let it not be the outward adorning...But let it be the hidden man of the heart, in that which is not corruptible, even the ornament of a meek and quiet spirit, which is the sight of God of great price.
1 Pet 3:3-4

Attention breeds affection; get informed before you get involved.

The righteous should choose his friends carefully.
Prov 12:26a

It is far better for a lady to make up her mind than to make up her face.

As a ring of gold in a swine's snout, so is a fair woman who is without discretion.
Prov 11:22

The ability to use less to accomplish more is an important feature of a desirable lady. No man wants to marry a liability, every man wants to marry an asset.

The heart of her husband doth safely trust in her, so that he shall have no need of spoil.
Prov 31:11

Never judge a thing by its first appearance. Face value is usually a false value. Insight is superior to mere sight.

But the Lord said unto Samuel, look not on his countenance, because I have refused him...for the Lord seeth not as a man seeth ;for man looketh on the outward appearance, but the Lord looketh on the heart.
1Sam 16:7

It takes a real man to unwrap this gift delicately veiled in feminity called you.

Wherefore henceforth know we no man after the flesh: yea, though we have known Christ after the flesh, yet now henceforth know we him no more.
2Cor 5:16

A man who lacks an understanding of your needs as a woman would not know what to fill in, in order to fulfill you.

Most men will proclaim every one his own goodness: but a faithful man who can find?
Pro 20:6

A woman who is not defined is a woman that will be defiled.

Butter and honey shall he eat, that he may know to refuse the evil, and choose the good.
Isa 7:15

To be double without trouble, you must first be a single without wrinkles. It is that simple.

If the foundations are destroyed, What can the righteous do?
Psalm 11:3 NKJV

There are two sides to love: devotion and romance.

Let her be as the loving and pleasant roe: let her breast satisfy thee at all times; and be thou ravished always with her love.
Prov 5:19

Devotion without romance can be boring. Romance without devotion can be heart breaking .It takes both to have a heaven on earth relationship.

Let the husband render unto his wife due benevolence; and likewise also the wife unto the husband.
1Cor 7:3

Many Children are born, few are raised. Raise your own!

Train up a child in the way he should go; and when he is old, he will not depart from it.
Prov 22:6

To lecture a child is to leave the responsibility of discovery to him. To teach him is to show him the way. To train him is to show him the way, go through yourself and then take him through.

Those things, which ye have learned and received and heard and seen in me, do.
Phil 4:9

The greatest honour in life is to be called a father. It means you are sharing a name with the Almighty God. But it is also the greatest responsibility.

Lo, children are an heritage of the Lord, and the fruits of the womb is the reward. Happy is the man that hath his quiver full of them.
Psalms 127:3-5

Training precedes reigning. A child not trained cannot reign.

Train up a child in the way he should go; and when he is old, he would not depart from it.
Prov 22:6

GRATITUDE

A man that is not grateful is a great fool.

Oh that men would praise the Lord, for his goodness and for his wonderful works to the children of men.
Psalm 107:8

The spirit of gratitude is your access to higher altitude. Those that praise God will be raised up.

Were there not ten cleansed? There are not found that returned to give glory to God, save this stranger.
Luke 17:17-18.

If you will testify, He will glorify.
Appreciation is the application for more.

Let the people praise thee... O God...Then shall the earth yield her increase and God, even our God shall bless us.
Psalm 67: 5-6.

LAWS OF HARVEST

Giving precedes being given.

Give, and it shall be given unto you.
Luke 6:38

To succeed you must sow seeds.

Then Isaac sowed in that land, and received in the same year an hundred fold; and the Lord blessed him. And the man waxed great, and went forward, and grew until he became very great.
Gen 26:12-13

Until your seed finds its field, you will never know its full potential to yield.

But others fell into good ground, and brought forth fruit, some an hundred fold, some sixty-fold, some thirty fold.
Matt 13:8

Love is a seed and not a risk. If you must reap it, then you must generously sow it.

A man who has friends must himself be friendly.
Prov. 18:24a NKJV

God will only allow to flow to you what you allow to flow through you.

Be not deceived, God is not mocked; for whatsoever a man soweth, that shall he also reap.
Gal 6:7

Time is your greatest opportunity for significance. To invest it, is to harvest seasons of great rewards.

Redeeming the time because the days are evil.
Eph 5:16

What you cannot give is an idol. What you cannot give, you will worship.

You cannot serve God and mammon.
Matthew 6:24b

PRODUCTIVITY

The genesis of your dominion lies in your productivity.

And God blessed them, and God said unto them, Be fruitful and multiply, and replenish the earth ,and subdue it ;and have dominion over the fish of the sea ,and over the fowl of the air ,and every other living thing that moveth upon the earth.
Gen 1:28

A man that will not produce is a life tenant. He is a silent curse upon his generation. He carries daily a virus called failure.

Behold these three years I come seeking fruit on this fig tree, and find none; cut it down; why cumbereth it the ground?
Luke 13:7

You will never have the power to perform in what you lack the passion to pursue.

for it is God who works in you both to will and to do for His good pleasure.
Phil 2:13

Utility enhances Productivity. Stir up the gift of God in you.

Wherefore I put thee in remembrance that thou stir up the gift of God, which is in thee by the putting on of my hands.
2Tim 1:6

Every intention that is deprived of attention suffers in detention.

Wherefore the rather, brethren, give diligence to make thy calling and election sure; for if ye do these things you shall never fall.
2Pet 1:10

Our civil service system needs to be more challenging, its current outlook reinforces lethargy. We promote people based on duration, not on donation, but we must realize that longevity is not the same as productivity.

And all the days of methuselah were nine hundred and nine years; and he died.
Gen 5: 27

Longevity is not equal to productivity. Tenure is not the same as impact.

And all the days of methuselah were nine hundred and nine years; and he died.
Gen 5: 27

FAITH AND PATIENCE

Faith and Patience are two inseparable virtues, it takes both to receive God's best.

That ye be not slothful, but followers of them who through faith and patience inherit the promise.
Heb 6:12

The creation of the world is a revelation of the God of timing, the God of order, the God of beauty and the God of patience.

He hath made everything beautiful in his time.
Eccl 3:11a

Promise delayed is not promise denied.

For the vision is yet for an appointed time; But at the end it will speak, and it will not lie. Though it tarries, wait for it; Because it will surely come, It will not tarry.
Hab. 2:3

It takes faith and patience to receive God's best. Faith without patience usually results in accidents.

For ye have need of patience that after ye have done the will of God, ye might receive the promise.
Heb 10:36

Don't mistake God's test for Satan's superiority.

Submit yourself therefore to God, resist the devil and he will flee from you.
James 4:7

All men face mountains, but the ones with faith move theirs.

for verily I say unto you, if ye have faith as a grain of mustard seed, ye shall say unto this mountain ,remove hence to yonder place ,and it shall remove ,and nothing shall be impossible unto you.
Matt 17:20

I know your mountain is about to move by the things you are saying.

For verily I say unto you, That whosoever shall say unto this mountain, Be thou removed, and be thou cast into the sea; and shall not doubt in his heart, but shall believe that those things which he saith shall come to pass; he shall have whatsoever he saith.
Mar 11:23

Christianity is about believing, becoming and belonging.

But without faith, it is impossible to please him; for he that cometh to God must believe that he is, and he is a rewarder of them that diligently seek him.
Heb 11:6

COMMITMENT AND UNDERSTANDING

Understanding is the matrix of manifestation.

And they that understand among the people shall instruct many.
Dan 11:33a

To get committed, stay connected.

And Ruth said, Intreat me not to leave thee, or to return from following after thee: for whither thou goest, I will go; and where thou lodgest, I will lodge: thy people shall be my people, and thy God my God.
Ruth 1:16

The difference between the successful and the failure is commitment.

Meditate upon these things, give thyself wholly to them, that thy profiting may appear to all.
1Tim 4:15

Understanding makes you outstanding in life.

And of the men of Issachar, which were men that had understanding of the times, to know what Israel ought to do; the heads of them were two hundred; and all the brethren were at their commandment.
1chr 12:32

RESPONSIBILITY

You do not have power over your birth place, but you do have it over your future abode, both here and hereafter. Exercise it well.

I was no prophet, neither was I a prophet's son but I was a herdsman, and a gatherer of sycamore fruit: And the Lord took me as I followed the flock and the LORD said unto me, go prophesy unto my people Israel.
Amos 7:14-15

God-inspired dreams are just like babies. A baby may stagger but please let him live. Give growth a chance!

And the child grew and was in the desert till the day of his shewing unto Israel.
Luke 1:80b

The privilege of life is worthy of celebration, but the pleasure of life lies in the achievements.

There's nothing better for a man than that he should eat and drink, and that he should make his soul enjoy good in his labour. This also i saw, that it was from the hand of God.
Eccl 2:24

He supplies the grace, we run the race. He supplies the oil, we do the burning. He supplies the light, we do the shining.

But by the grace of God, I am what I am; and his grace which was bestowed upon me was not in vain; but I laboured more abundantly than they all; yet not I, but the grace of God which was with me.
1 Cor 15:10.

Whatever we can visualize, we can actualize.

For all the land which thou seest, to thee will I give it,
And to thy seed forever.
Gen 13:15.

God never made industries, nor built houses, He only made man and left man to create the rest.

And on the seventh day, God ended from all his work, which he had made; and he rested on the seventh day from all his work, which he had made.
Gen 2:2

Give drive to your dreams. Every dream that lacks drive becomes drowned.

Wherefore the rather, brethren, give diligence to make your calling and election sure; for if ye do these things, ye shall never fall.
2Pet 1:10

Whatever you assist to persist in your mind will ultimately exist in your life. Guard your heart with all diligence.

Keep thy heart with all diligence; for out of it (are) the issues of life.
Prov 4:23

The seeds of greatness are Vision and Passion; that is, direction and intense pursuit.

And the LORD answered me, and said ,Write the vision ,and make it plain upon tables ,that he may run that readeth it. For the vision is yet for an appointed time, but at the end it shall speak, and not lie; though it tarry, wait for it; because it will surely come, it will not tarry.
Hab 2:2-3

Some make History, others read it. Some make it glow, others watch it glow.

Let your light so shine before men, that they may see your good works and glorify your Father in heaven.
Matt 5:16 NKJV

God gives you today, but promises you tomorrow. He expects you to use what you have been given to realize what you have been promised.

I call heaven and earth to record this day against you, that I have set before you life and death, blessing and cursing: therefore choose life, that both thou and thy seed may live.
Deu 30:19

The only way to realize tomorrow is to maximize today.

See then that ye walk circumspectly, not as fools, but as wise, Redeeming the time.
Eph 5:15-16

If you walk out of God's will, you will walk into Life's ills.

There is a way that seemeth right unto a man but the end thereof are the ways of death ...the man that wandereth out of the way of understanding shall remain in the congregation of the dead.
Prov 16:25; 21:16

The word "impossible"
is restricted to the world
of the irresponsible.
When ability rises up to
responsibility, all things
always become possible.

Jesus said unto him, if thou canst believe, all things are possible to him that believeth.
Mark 9:23

PRAYER AND THE WORD

Prayer is for power generation. It is the mother of events.

And when they had prayed, the place was shaken where they were assembled together ...for as soon as Zion travailed, she brought forth her children.
Acts 4:31, Isa 66:8

To succeed in life, you need more than the knowledge of science, you need the knowledge of the Omniscient.

But the people that do know their God shall be strong and do exploits.
Dan 11:32b

Jesus never taught his disciples how to preach, He only taught them how to pray. Why? Knowing how to talk to God is more important than knowing how to talk to men.

After this manner therefore pray ye: Our father which art in heaven, Hallowed be thy name.
Matt 6:9.

Prayer increases your influence. Any place you have reached in the Spirit, in the place of prayer, you will eventually reach in the physical realm. It is only a matter of time.

Thine eyes shall see the king in his beauty: they shall behold the land that is very far off.
Isa 33:17

In life, outside warfare,
don't expect a
thoroughfare.

And from the days of John the Baptist until now, the kingdom of heaven suffereth violence, and the violent take it by force.
Matt 11:12

To travail is to prevail, to travail is to triumph.

And he said, Thy name shall be called no more Jacob, but Israel: for as a prince hast thou power with God and with men, and hast prevailed.
Gen 32:28

The word you cannot declare cannot give you the world that you desire.

By faith we understand that the worlds were framed by the word of God, so that the things which are seen were not made of things which are visible.
Heb 11:3

Knowledge not updated would make you outdated. therefore, a step upward in knowledge is a step forward in life.

A wise man is strong; yea a man of knowledge increaseth strength.
Prov 24:5

No man can be more than what grace makes him.

But by the grace of God I am what I am; and His grace which was bestowed upon me was not in vain; but I labored more abundantly than they all; yet not I, but the grace of God which was with me.
1Cor 15:10

If it is God's word, it will always produce God's result.

So shall my word be that goeth forth out of my mouth; it shall not return unto me void, but it shall accomplish that which I please ,and it shall prosper in the thing whereunto I sent it.
Isa 55:11

Every problem contains the seed of its own solution, every trial the seed for triumphs, every obstacle the seed for miracles.

There hath no temptation taken you but such as is common to man; but God is faithful, who will not suffer you to be tempted above that ye are able, but will with the temptation also make a way to escape, that ye may be able to bear it.
1 cor 10:13

Prayer does not call for decency, it only calls for fervency. So pray!

Who in the days of his flesh, when he had offered up prayers and supplications with strong crying and tears unto him that was able to save him from death ,and was heard in that he feared.
Heb 5:7

Your mountain can reduce in size, only if you increase in revelation.

And wisdom and knowledge shall be the stability of thy times and the strength of salvation.
Isa 33:6a

Prayer is agonizing in the realm of the spirit for success in the realm of the natural.

The effectual fervent prayer of a righteous man availeth much.
Jas 5:16

Prayer gives you access to the Omnipotence of God.

Ask, and it shall be given unto you; seek and ye shall find; knock and it shall be opened unto you: Then Hezekiah turned his face toward the wall and prayed unto the Lord.
Matt 7:7&, Isa 38:2.

Answers are dependent on Prayers. You have not because you ask not.

Ye lust and have not: ye kill and desire to have, and cannot obtain: ye fight and war, yet ye have not, because ye ask not.
James 4:2

Prayer turns difficulties into possibilities.

But in everything by prayer and supplication with thanksgiving, let your requests be made known unto God. And the peace of God...shall keep your hearts and minds.
Phil 4:6-7

CONCLUSION

Success requires that you believe in God who is the giver of dreams, Believe in yourself the dreamer, And believe in your dreams. For you must believe to achieve, and you must believe to become.

FIRST THINGS FIRST

Man was created with an instinct to worship, fellowship and dominate. You sure need God in your life. The greatest decision you can ever make is to accept the Lordship of Jesus into your life as this has an implication on your life here on earth and hereafter. Have you accepted Jesus into your life? Are you born again? If you are not sure, say these words:

"Lord Jesus, I believe you died on the cross, and was buried and rose again from death because of me. I come to you today. I am a sinner and cannot help myself. Forgive me my sins. Cleanse me with your blood. Today, I accept You as my Lord and Saviour. Thank you for saving me. Amen.

Dear friend, welcome to the family of God. Be free to be a part of God's people around you.

I will love to read from you.

E-mail: reveboda@gmail.com

Twitter: @niyieboda Facebook: Gbeminiyi Eboda

OTHER BOOKS BY THE AUTHOR

SEE OVERLEAF

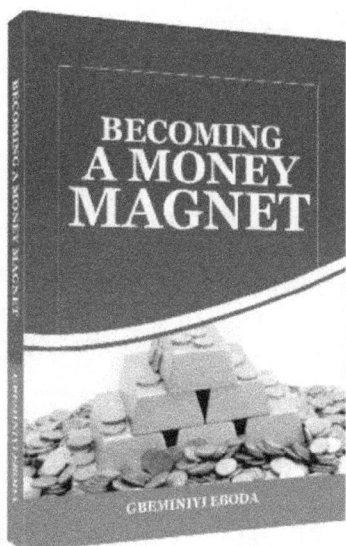

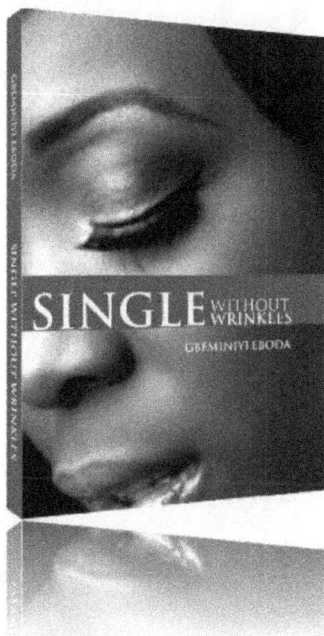

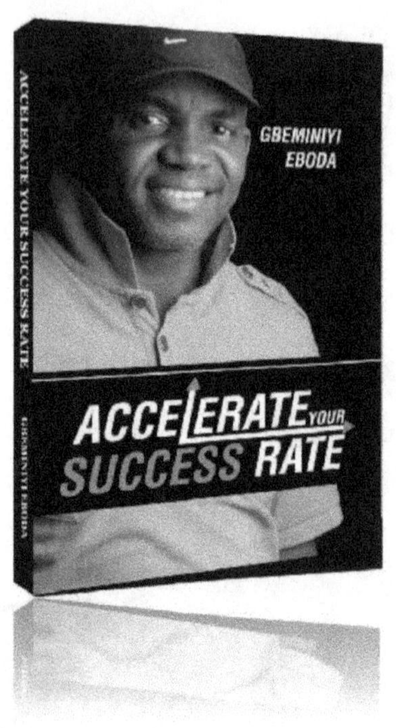

"The impossible is the untried". This book is suitable for individuals and organisations who will dare the odds and venture the impossible to become more and do more and ultimately have more.

This text is another archetypal to guide you from living a life of activity into a life of higher productivity!

There's no barrier to success. It's all about you. This book will help you find a way out of ignorance and develop a very strong database that will usher you into the future that you have always dreamt of.

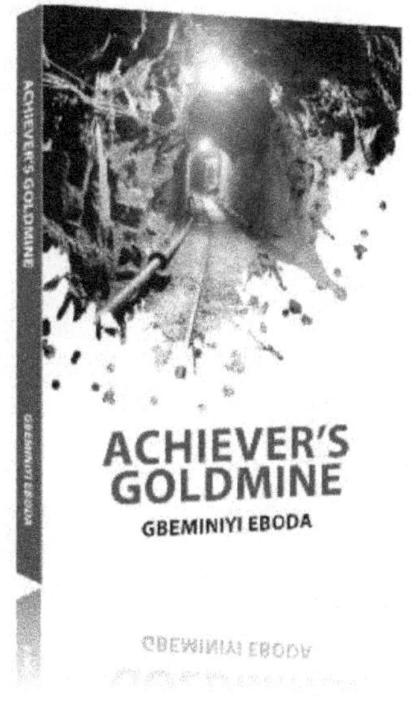

You are the main character in this book! This text is a blue-print or guide which if followed will take you from where you are to where you want and passionately desire to be in life and the whole concept is to help unearth the value on your inside from its potential form.

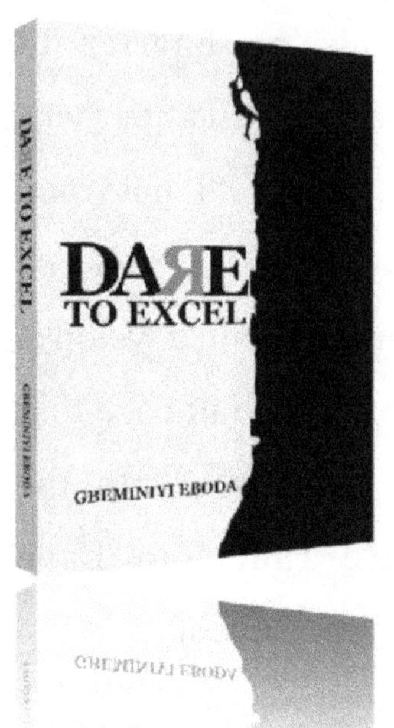

Success requires that you believe in God, yourself and the dream. These are wisdom tips packaged for a forward-focused dreamer on his way to achieving greatness.

www.ingramcontent.com/pod-product-compliance
Lightning Source LLC
Chambersburg PA
CBHW020506030426
42337CB00011B/250
9789783774209